CRICKET

Gill Lloyd
and
David Jefferis

Wayland

SPORTS SKILLS

Cricket	Netball
Gymnastics	Rugby Union
Hockey	Soccer
Judo	Tennis

Photographs by Roger Wootton, *Cricket World,* Action Plus, All Sport
Illustrations by James Robins and Drawing Attention
Consultant Andy Lloyd, National Cricket Association Advanced Coach

This edition published in 1995 by
Wayland (Publishers) Ltd

First published in 1993 by
Wayland (Publishers) Ltd
61 Western Road, Hove
East Sussex BN3 1JD, England

© Copyright 1993 Wayland (Publishers) Limited

British Library Cataloguing in Publication Data
Lloyd, Gill
   Cricket. - (Sports Skills Series)
   I. Title II. Jefferis, David
   III. Robins, James IV. Series
   796.358

HARDBACK ISBN 0-7502-0875-9

PAPERBACK ISBN 0-7502-1700-6

DTP by The Design Shop
Printed and bound in Italy by G. Canale & C.S p.A., Turin

Contents

Introduction

Cricket is one of the most enjoyable games of all time. It is popular with both young and older people, boys and girls, players and spectators. It offers a combination of the skills of hitting a ball, running, catching and throwing. Although it is a competitive team game for eleven players, it is also a great test of individual skill and performance.

Cricket can be played at lots of different levels, depending on the standard of players and the amount of time available for a game. Cricket clubs tend to play afternoon cricket. Many have junior sections that welcome enthusiastic newcomers to their coaching sessions.

◁ Finding good young players is an important priority for most cricket clubs. Young batsmen can be taught to play their shots correctly and be given a chance to practise their skills.

At the highest level of cricket, five-day test matches and one-day internationals are played between the major cricket-playing nations of the world - England, Australia, West Indies, India, Pakistan, New Zealand, Sri Lanka, South Africa and Zimbabwe. These games are followed closely by millions of cricket supporters.

△ The wicketkeeper leaps for the ball, in this exciting Women's World Cup match between England and Australia. Top women players take part in one-day internationals and test series.

Field, pitch and wicket

Cricket can be played on a field of any shape or size, but the grass should be mown and the outer boundary must be clearly marked. The action of the game centres on the pitch - the strip in the centre of the field. The wickets are positioned directly opposite each other at the ends of the pitch. Each wicket is made up of three wooden stumps with two wooden bails balanced on top of them. The distance between the wickets is usually 20.12 m (22 yards) but is shortened to 16.5 or 17.4 m (18 or 19 yards) for players under eleven years.

Field and pitch

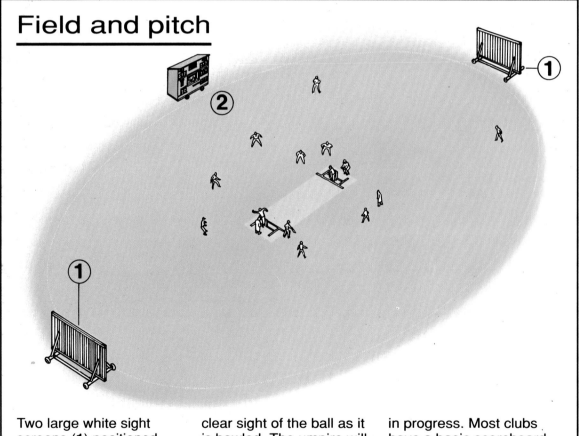

Two large white sight screens (1) positioned outside the boundary behind each wicket help a batsman be sure of a clear sight of the ball as it is bowled. The umpire will stop play if spectators cross in front of a sightscreen while play is in progress. Most clubs have a basic scoreboard (2) which gives general information about the state of play.

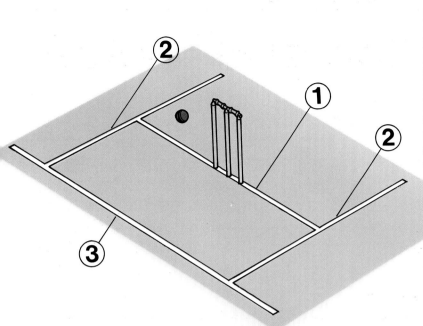

◁ The lines marked on the pitch in front of the wicket are called creases. The bowling crease (**1**) and the return creases (**2**) show the bowler where to place his or her feet when delivering a ball. The popping crease (**3**) shows the batsman where to stand while waiting for a delivery and where to reach when taking a run.

▷ Because the ball bounces on the pitch, the condition of the surface is of great interest to players. Is it grassy, damp, dry or worn? Dry hard pitches, for example, tend to favour fast bowlers, whereas a damp pitch slows balls down. Grass like that in the picture is normally mown and rolled flat before a game.

Kit and equipment

Cricket is traditionally played in all-white clothing. Shirts and sweaters are worn on top, with trousers for boys and skirts for girls. A good pair of cricket shoes is important. They should have spiked soles and allow room for wearing a pair of woollen socks.

The cricket bat is a key piece of equipment. It needs to be well-balanced and not too heavy for you. A bat that is too long or too heavy will stop you from learning your batting strokes correctly. As a general guide, you should be able to lift your bat easily with just one hand. It is better to have a shortish handle on your bat while you are learning.

◁ The ball is hard in cricket and at times all batsmen get knocks, so protective clothing is essential. Helmets are now an accepted part of protective equipment. They are worn by batsmen and close-in fielders. This batsman (England player, Chris Lewis) also wears a thigh protector.

▷ Janette Brittain of England. Notice how her legs look comfortable in batting pads, with her knees fitting exactly into the roll of the pad.

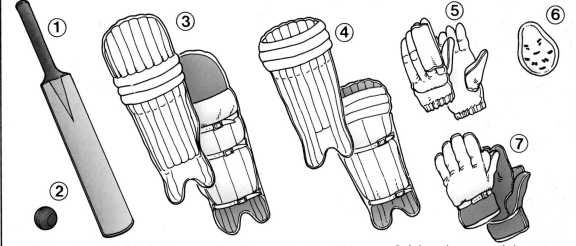

1 Bats are available in junior sizes.
2 Balls are made of cork, bound with twine and cased in red leather with a seam stitched around the middle.

3 Batting pads should be light and comfortable so that you can run easily.
4 Wicketkeeper's pads are shorter.
5 Choose batting gloves with rolled padding.

6 A box is essential equipment for boys as soon as they start playing with a hard cricket ball.
7 Wicketkeeping gloves should fit snugly, allowing hands to move easily.

Rules and scoring

Teams take it in turns to bat (take their innings) or field. The fielding side has all its players on the field, but only two batsmen, one at each wicket, play at a time. The aim is to score runs, either by running between the wickets or by hitting the ball far. The game is controlled by two umpires. One stands by the bowler's wicket, the other facing the batsman's wicket. They use a number of signals to communicate their decisions.

If you hit the ball you can run if you choose to. You may run as many times as you can before the ball is returned by the fielders to one or other of the wickets. If the ball crosses the boundary there is no need to run as this counts as four runs. If it crosses the boundary without touching the ground first, it counts as six runs.

Umpire's signals

The umpire signals a four (**1**) a six (**2**) and out (**3**). When running, you and the batsman at the other wicket both have to cross and ground your bat in the opposite popping crease, or the umpire will call a short run (**4**) and the run does not count.

A bye (**5**) and a leg-bye (**6**) are runs scored from balls that have not hit the bat. A no-ball (see page 13) (**7**) and a wide (see page 31) (**8**) are considered illegal or unfair balls. Each no-ball and wide is worth an extra run to the other side. Runs from byes, leg byes, no-balls and wides are called extras. Extras are added to the batting side's overall score.

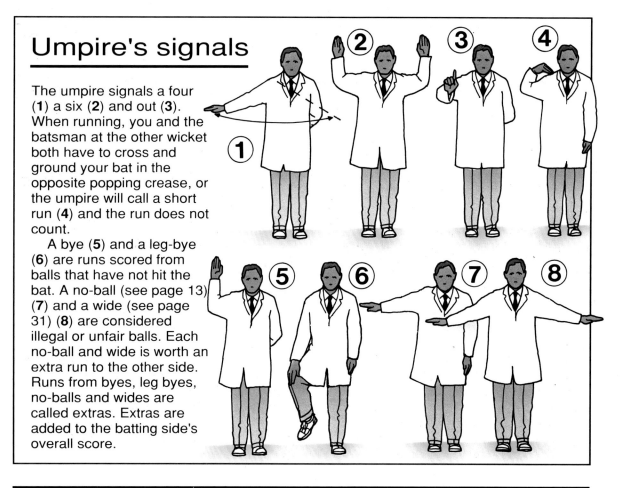

▷ Pakistan bowler, Wasim Akram, appeals to the umpire for an LBW decision (see below). Unless a member of the fielding side asks 'How's that?' the umpire cannot decide a player is out. In this case the umpire has raised his finger to signal the player is indeed out.

Imagine when you are batting that you are guarding your wicket and your only weapon is your bat. The fielding side is trying to get you out, but it is the umpire who makes the decision. There are eleven possible ways of getting out, but these six examples are the most common ones:

Bowled
When a fair ball breaks your wicket and dislodges your bails.

Hit wicket
If you knock the bails off yourself while batting. You won't be out though, if you knock the bails off while running.

Stumped
If you are out of your crease while making a stroke and the wicketkeeper knocks the bails off with the ball in his or her hands.

Caught
If a fielder catches a ball you have hit before it touches the ground.

Run out
If you don't ground your bat in the opposite popping crease before a fielder breaks the wicket with the ball.

Leg Before Wicket (LBW)
If you stop a fair ball that would have hit your wicket with anything other than your bat.

Bowling 1

One of the most satisfying skills of cricket is bowling. It takes time and lots of practice to develop a smooth and accurate bowling action, but the rewards of getting a batsman out with an accurately-delivered ball make it all worthwhile.

The first rule is to hold the ball in your fingers, not in the palm of your hand. Although your grip may need to change for different types of bowling, the basic grip should be mastered first.

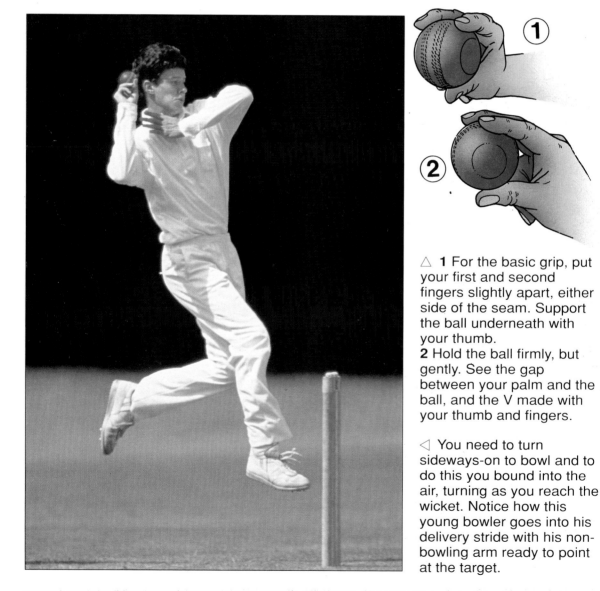

△ **1** For the basic grip, put your first and second fingers slightly apart, either side of the seam. Support the ball underneath with your thumb.
2 Hold the ball firmly, but gently. See the gap between your palm and the ball, and the V made with your thumb and fingers.

◁ You need to turn sideways-on to bowl and to do this you bound into the air, turning as you reach the wicket. Notice how this young bowler goes into his delivery stride with his non-bowling arm ready to point at the target.

Bowling action

The run-up, illustrated here for a right-handed player, gives you the basic rhythm. Fix your eyes on the spot you plan to aim for, lengthen your stride and increase your pace as you run in.

1 As you reach the wicket, turn your body sideways with a bound on your last pace.

2 Your left shoulder should point towards the batsman, your left arm high above your head, weight on your back foot and body leaning away from the batsman.

3 As your left leg lands bend it slightly to absorb the impact and let your left arm pull your body into its delivery stride.

4 Bring your right arm over straight and high as you release the ball.

5 Your bowling arm follows through, swinging across your body so that your right shoulder points down the wicket.

Bowlers take turns, bowling in overs. An over consists of six fair deliveries from one end of the pitch. At the end of an over the batsmen remain where they are and another bowler delivers balls from the other end of the pitch. No bowler can bowl one over immediately after another. A series of overs is called a spell.

Some rules about bowling need to be followed or the umpire will signal a no-ball. You must not throw the ball, meaning that your arm must be straight when the ball leaves your hand. When you bowl, your back foot must be inside the return crease, your front foot not past the popping crease.

Bowling 2

1 Full toss reaches the batsman without bouncing.
2 Yorker lands close to the batsman's feet.
3 Half volley can be reached just as it hits the ground.
4 Good length ball has the batsman not sure whether to play back or forward to it.
5 Short length ball usually gives a batsman time to play a shot.
6 Bouncer is a fast, short-pitched ball that bounces chest-high or higher.

△ The speed or pace of bowling can be varied. A fast ball (Allan Donald is shown in action here) gives the batsman less time to think about shots. On the other hand, a spinning slow ball can catch even the best batsman out.

Good line and length are the sign of a capable bowler. The length of the ball is its distance from the batsman when it bounces or pitches. The skill of varying the length of balls to surprise batsmen is a useful one to practise. The line of bowling is the path a ball takes after it leaves the bowler's hand. A ball with a good line will hit the wicket.

You may have noticed bowlers rubbing the ball. This is to make it shine, because polishing one side of the ball helps it to swing in flight. The direction in which you point the seam of the ball is the other important factor. In spin bowling, the ball is said to turn as it lands on the pitch. In off-spin the ball pitches on the off side and turns in towards the wicket. In leg-spin the plan is to make the ball turn the opposite way, from the leg to the off side.

△ For off-spin, grip the ball so that your first finger lies across the seam, with its top joint slightly bent. This is the finger that does the spinning.

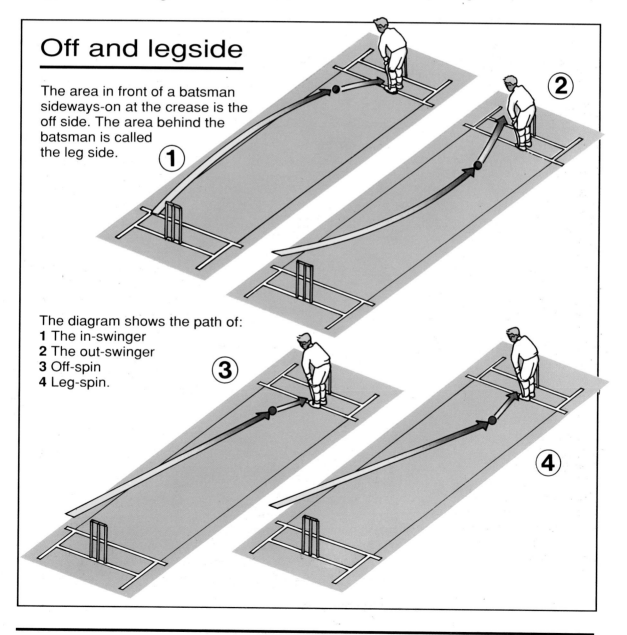

Off and legside

The area in front of a batsman sideways-on at the crease is the off side. The area behind the batsman is called the leg side.

①

②

The diagram shows the path of:
1 The in-swinger
2 The out-swinger
3 Off-spin
4 Leg-spin.

③ ④

Batting 1

The skill of batting lies in being able to see the ball, to know where it is going and when it will get there. You must judge its line, length and speed, choose the right stroke and play it with correct timing. You can learn a lot by watching good players in action, but never be afraid of hitting a ball in your own natural way.

There are various batting strokes, but all rely on a good grip, relaxed and comfortable stance, and a smooth backlift. The diagrams below and on other pages are for right-handed players.

Grip, stance and backlift

1 Grip
Hold your bat to have control over shots and the power to play them. Hands should be close together near the top of the handle, fingers and thumbs wrapped around it. The V-shapes made by your thumbs and first fingers should be in line with each other.

2 Stance
Your stance is the ready-and-waiting position. You should be evenly balanced with your feet on either side of the popping crease, knees slightly bent and your front shoulder pointing at the bowler. Your eyes should be level, your head slightly over your feet.

3 Backlift
Take your bat back straight, letting your wrists cock naturally. Keep your head still and your balance steady. Pick up your bat as the bowler's arm starts its upward swing. If your backlift is late your stroke will be hurried.

When you start batting, or change ends the first time, you need to ask the umpire to give you a 'guard' so that you know exactly where your bat is in relation to the wicket.

You could choose middle, middle-and-leg, or leg stump. The best guard is that which places your nose in line with middle stump, eyes level. Mark the ground so you can line up with it when facing the bowler.

△ Graham Hick, perfectly balanced and ready to play his shot. Notice how his front foot is starting to move into line with the ball.

Batting 2

You don't need to score runs off every ball, and it is useful to know some defensive or 'stopping' strokes, that are for playing safe and staying in play. Remember to watch the ball and keep your bat as straight as possible. For defensive strokes keep your top hand in front so that the angle of the bat hits the ball safely downwards and not up into the air for a catch.

◁ **Back defensive shot**
Move your rear foot back towards the stumps, in line with the ball. Keep your feet parallel to the crease. Keep your bat square to the ball and angle it downwards. The ball should hit your bat beneath your eyes. Your top elbow should be high, your bottom hand relaxed. The bat should be still as it meets the ball, which should drop to the ground.

▽ **Forward defensive shot**
Lead with your head and shoulders, to bring your front foot alongside the line of the ball. Bring the bat down straight, close to your front pad, to meet the ball directly under your eyes. Let your front knee bend slightly to take your weight. At the end of the stroke your body should be balanced and still, with the bat alongside your front pad.

▷ Drives are some of the most satisfying scoring shots a batsman can play. The drive begins exactly the same way as the forward defensive shot, but this time you swing through the line of the ball with firm hands, to give the shot power. Here, Robin Smith leans into this powerful off-drive in a one-day international match. For these exciting events, players wear coloured clothing. For action on television, a miniaturized TV camera can be mounted inside the middle stump.

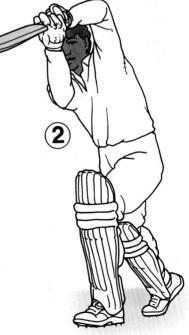

△ **Front-foot drive**

1 Lead with your head and shoulders to bring your front foot alongside the line of the ball. Swing your bat down, to meet the ball level with your front foot, and directly under your eyes.

2 Continue to swing your bat through to finish pointing down the line in which the ball has been hit. Your body ends up balanced with most of its weight on your front foot.

Batting 3

The hit to leg, or 'pull shot', is an easy and natural stroke to play when you first start cricket, because most balls bounce quite high. You will find this a good scoring shot. The square cut is a useful shot to play to all short-pitched balls outside the off-stump.

The pull

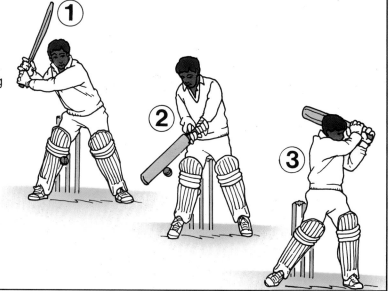

1 Move your right foot back towards the stumps, turning it to point down the pitch. Bring your left foot level with the right, head in line with the ball, body facing down the pitch.
2 Bring the bat down to meet the ball at arm's length.
3 At the end of the stroke your weight ends up on your front foot, as you follow through.

The square cut

1 Move your rear foot back and across to the stumps, pointing to gully (see page 27).
2 Sweep your bat down and across to meet the ball at arm's length.
3 Nearly all your weight should now be on your back foot. Your wrists roll over naturally as you make a good follow through.

Good running between the wickets is one of the skills of batting. As soon as you hit the ball you have to decide whether to run or not. It is important to be positive. Call 'yes', 'no' or 'wait', followed quickly by the decision. Dithering and changing your mind can get the other batsman out. But call only for balls that you can see. If the ball has gone behind your back it is the other batsman who should call.

The call for the second or third run is usually made by the person running towards the wicket at which the ball is likely to be thrown.

△ Always run at full speed, sliding the bat along the ground with your arm stretched out, as you get near the popping crease.

Fielding

Good fielding is very important to the success of a team, and all cricketers need to be good at catching, stopping and throwing a ball. You can improve your fielding by learning to relax when the ball is out of play and really concentrating when the ball is 'live'. You can guess what's about to happen by looking at the right things. Watch the ball as it leaves the bowler's hand, watch the batsman's feet to see what stroke is about to be played, and look at the bat to pick up the path of the ball.

Catching

1 Close catching
Get into a crouching position, feet apart, weight evenly spread. Your hands should be forward and together, with palms facing the ball, fingers pointing down. Let your hands give as you take the ball.

2 High catching
Get sight of the ball before you move. Then move into position to catch the ball in front of your eyes. Keep your fingers wide, palms facing the ball. Let your hands give as you take the ball. Hold the ball near your chest.

3 Pick up and return
Move into the line of the ball. Drop down on one leg, left knee in line with the ball, the other leg at right-angles. Gather the ball in your hands, in fingers-down position, in front of your left knee. Watch the ball all the way into your hands. Take one step, aim and throw.

Accurate throwing is an important fielding skill and it is worth practising your throwing technique. For long-distance throws, use a lofted overarm action. For medium distances use a shoulder level throw. For speed and short distances, including throws at the stumps, throw underarm. Don't run in with a ball if you are on the boundary - throw the ball flat, so it bounces in front of the keeper.

Remember, you should always back up other fielders particularly when a return is being made to the wicket. A poor throw or a misfield may lead to extra runs being taken. These are known as overthrows.

△ A brilliant diving catch, taken by a close-in fielder. Catches such as these are the result of total concentration and lightning-fast reactions.

Wicketkeeping

Wicketkeeping appeals to the sort of player who likes to be totally involved in a game the whole time.

Stand right up to the wicket for slow bowling and well back for fast bowling. If you take up a middle position the ball will come through at an awkward height. Sighting the ball properly is essential. For standing up you will have your inside foot in line with middle or off-stump; for standing back you will be just outside the line of off-stump.

Assume that every ball is coming through to you. Don't grab or snatch at the ball, get into line by moving your feet in a sideways shuffle and let the ball come to you. Your hands should give as the ball reaches them.

△ The wicketkeeper takes up a crouching position behind the stumps with weight on the balls of both feet. Her hands are close together, the fingertips are pointing down, and the palms face the bowler.

Once you have the ball, bring it to the top of the stumps, and keep it there in case of a stumping chance. A stumping will only be possible when you are standing up to a slowish bowler. If the batsman starts advancing up the wicket to meet a ball and misses it, try to take the ball and break the wicket all in one swift movement. Don't be tempted to snatch at the ball. Remember you have to take the ball cleanly before you break the wicket.

△ If the batsman hits the ball, get up to the wicket and be ready to receive the throw from a fielder. You might have a chance of a run out if you can break the wicket with the ball before the batsman grounds the bat over the popping crease.

Captaincy and tactics

Each team is led by a captain. The other players of the team look to their captain for leadership, guidance and encouragement. A captain's jobs include: choosing whether to bat or bowl first; deciding on the batting order; deciding who bowls and when; organizing fielding positions; keeping the team aware of tactics and deciding when to declare the end to an innings.

At the start of play, the captains of each team come on to the pitch and toss a coin, to decide which team will bat first.

A captain with a strong bowling side may put the other team in to bat first, hoping to get them all out for a small score. If a captain has a strong batting side he or she may want to bat first, hoping to make a big score which the other side will find difficult to beat.

△ To make the best use of bowling strength, the tactic may be to attack, keeping fielders in close positions for as long as possible. This keeps the pressure on batsmen, as they dare not make mistakes.

△ Australian captain, Allan Border, moves his fielders.

Fielding positions

1 First slip
2 Second slip
3 Third slip
4 Gully
5 Silly point
6 Short extra cover
7 Silly mid-off
8 Silly mid-on
9 Short leg
10 Forward short-leg
11 Backward short-leg
12 Wicketkeeper

13 Mid-on
14 Mid-wicket
15 Square-leg
16 Backward square-leg
17 Short fine-leg
18 Short third-man
19 Backward point

20 Point
21 Mid-off
22 Deep mid-off
23 Long off
24 Deep mid-on
25 Long on
26 Deep mid-wicket

27 Deep square-leg
28 Long leg
29 Deep fine-leg
30 Third man
31 Deep point
32 Extra cover
33 Deep extra

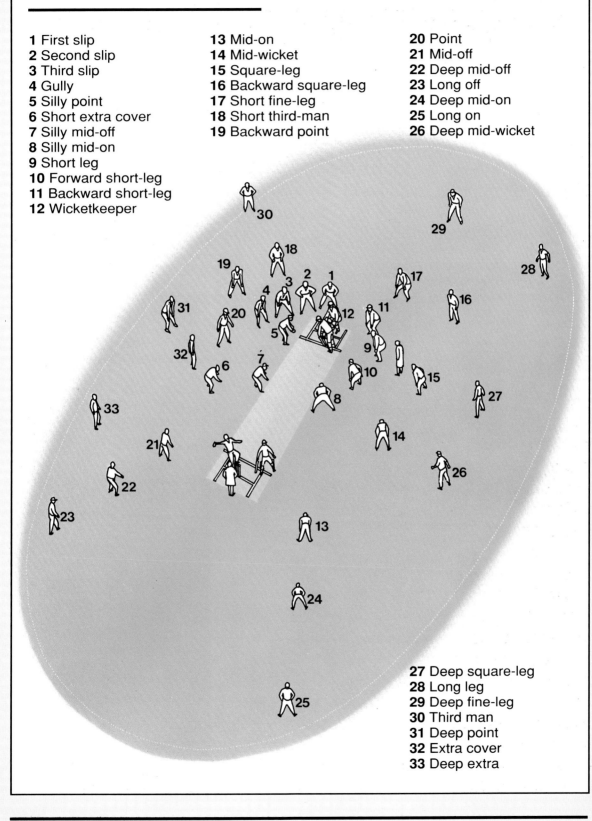

Indoor and kwik cricket

Indoor cricket is fast and exciting. It is a fairly new off-shoot of the outdoor game, and is particularly popular in Australia and New Zealand, where it is played at over 200 centres. In Britain too, its popularity is growing rapidly. Families and social groups tend to take part, rather than club cricketers, but this does not mean that it is any less competitive. The teams that play in the indoor cricket leagues are highly trained and skilled. Kwik cricket is a simplified game, designed for children, to be played inside or out.

◁ Indoor cricket is played eight-a-side on synthetic carpet, surrounded by netting. Each player bats for four overs and if he or she gets out, five runs are deducted from the score. Everyone bowls two overs. A softer ball is used, so protective clothing is not necessary.

▷ In recent years there have been a number of simplified cricket games developed for children. These games are designed to improve eye, hand and ball co-ordination skills, which are essential requirements for team play. One such game is shown here, the popular kwik cricket. Kanga is a similar type of game, also aimed at young players.

Glossary

Appeal
A shout of 'How's that?' to the umpire by one of the fielding side, asking for a batsman to be given out.

Backing-up
One fielder covering a team-mate in case of a misfield.

Break
A ball's movement from its straight course after bouncing.

Bouncer
A fast, short-pitched ball that reaches the batsman at shoulder height or higher.

Bye
A run scored from a ball that passes the wicket without touching the batsman or bat.

Creases
The lines on the pitch consisting of the bowling crease, popping crease and return creases.

Dead ball
A ball that is out of play. The ball is dead at the end of an over, when a batsman is out, when it is over the boundary or when it has reached the hands of the bowler or wicketkeeper at the wicket.

Declaration
The close of an innings by the batting side's captain.

Deep
The part of the field near the boundary.

Duck
A batting score of zero.

Extras
Any runs that result from no-balls, byes, leg byes and wides.

Fair ball
A ball that has been legally bowled.

Innings
The length of play a batting turn for a whole team takes.

Leg before wicket (LBW)
Getting out to a ball which the umpire judges has hit a part of the body, without hitting the bat first, and which would otherwise have hit the wicket.

Leg bye
A run from a ball that has come off some part of the batsman's body, other than the hand.

Leg side
The side of the pitch behind a batsman sideways-on at the crease. Also called 'on side'.

Limited-over match
A match in which the number of overs to be bowled by each side is agreed before the start.

Maiden over
An over from which no runs are scored.

No ball
An illegal bowling delivery.

Off side
The side of the field in front of the batsman standing sideways on at the crease.

On side
See leg side

Over
Six deliveries from one end by a bowler.

Overthrows
A throw to a fielder at the wicket that goes past him or her and so allows the batsmen to take more runs.

Sweep
A batting stroke made off the front foot with the knee of the back leg almost on the ground.

Wide
A ball that is indicated by the umpire to be too high or wide to be hit.

Yorker
A ball that pitches near the batsman's feet.

Books to read

Cricket, (World of Sport series) Peter Perchard (Wayland, 1988)
Cricket, (Play the Game series) Ian Morrison (Ward Lock, 1992)
Sportsmasters Cricket (The laws and rules made simple),
Gill Freeman (Cambridge University Press, 1984)

For teachers and coaches:
Cricket: Technique, Tactics, Training, Doug Ferguson
(The Crowood Press, 1992)

Index